INSIDE MY MIND

A Collection of Poems,
Short Stories,
and Life Observations
by Graham Thomson,
'The Parkie Poet'

Dedicated with continuing thanks to my amazing children Emma and Gary, who motivate me on my worst days to just complete a simple task.

Without their love and support, the two books I have written would have been impossible.

Positive outcomes only.

Contents

Parkinson's

The Parkie Walk

Are you walking the Parkie walk on your own?

You can do it brother you just have to be strong.

It won't be easy my friend.

Bumpy roads along the way

Reach out to those who care enough to help.

And don't ever turn them away.

When the fog comes

When the fog comes, and you can't clear your thoughts.

Your mind is blank.

And you can't see what should be obvious to you and me.

How long will it last?

And what if I can't tell

If it has lifted or not

Maybe this time it doesn't shift.

And this my friend is your lot.

If I knew the difference

It might be a terrible thought.

Parkinson's Dementia

When the body works

But the mind doesn't

That's hard.

When the mind works

But the body doesn't

That's hard.

When neither work

That's called.

Parkinson's Dementia

Two Parkies have a chat.

A lovely morning chewing the fat.

For those that don't know that means having

a chat

We talked about times gone by like two old men.

But we reminded ourselves we are still in our prime

And are both a long way off.

From facing the end

Good company and friends are like gold.

Whatever your age your never to old.

To laugh out loud and plan ahead

We both chuckled and agreed.

You're a long time dead.

Lunch with a Parkie

When two Parkies get together for lunch

You somehow have that instant connection.

It can be like looking in the mirror.

You get each other.

It's like two brothers from a different mother.

The bond will last a lifetime.

We both know the road ahead.

But it only makes it stronger.

We have already been through so much.

We have nothing more we dread.

The subjects that we laughed at you would have thought we were mad.

But you must be able to laugh at this cruel disease.

And simply be glad.

For the good times.

Like lunch with a fellow Parkie.

I Can't Remember.

I can't remember.

What can't you remember.

I don't know I forget.

How can you forget.

I don't know if I ever knew.

What is false and what is true.

The mind has incredible powers.

When it works well.

But when it slows down.

It's like an old car that has ran out of oil.

Or a kettle that never seems to boil.

If you could give it a yearly service.

Once a year.

You could be confident again.

And not filled with fear.

Parkinson's your body

Parkinson's when your body

Is willing but your mind is not.

And your mind is willing, but your body is not.

And quite often neither are willing.

So that takes care of today.

But that's ok.

A lifetime passes.

When family and friends

The people you love and would do anything for

Becomes smaller as each year goes past.

A lot of people jumped from the train.

They were never meant to last.

young and old they stay away.

It wouldn't matter what you say.

To be honest though its better this way

The ones who are left have bought a life ticket to be with you.

The rest just bought a single day return.

As one by one they upped and flew.

For different reasons I dare say

It makes no difference now they are away.

To those who bought the lifetime pass

My love for you will always last

Thank you for being part of my journey!

You don't look like you have Parkinson's.

If I had a pound when someone

Would say you don't look like you have Parkinson's.

Or you don't look like you're in pain.

Surely you only get that disease when you are very old.

Maybe it's not their fault.

Perhaps they are trying to be nice.

They might not know what to say to me.

But then what would I expect from them.

Why should I expect anything.

Why should it matter what people think.

The reality is that it doesn't matter at all.

So, what is the problem.

The issue here is Parkinson's messes with my mind.

With my thoughts.

Overthink things imagine scenarios that are not true.

Or based on any fact.

Delusions and hallucinations are common-place, but you can't see them.

I don't have a special mark on my face alert-ing the world.

What it can be like in my space.

If your friends with a Parkie before you speak or get cross with them.

Please cut them some slack.

Wheelchair Life the Perils

It is 1.26am here in the world's most beautiful city.

I wonder who else is awake. Depending on where you are in the world and what you are doing.

I have been in bed for 4 hours my leg and foot so painful I can't sleep or put weight on it.

My own fault for going out without using my electric wheelchair.

I was using my walker and tripped on the kerb and as we say locally ended up on the flair.

I have a busy morning lined up but to be fair, unless things dramatically improve, I'm going nowhere.

Angry with myself but I'm sure fellow parkies will agree.

We don't want to give in and try and be the best we can be.

Going to be a long night.

Sleep oh not again

Sleep why have you deserted me.

We got on quite well for a few days.

But here you are back in your own ways.

What did I do to make you change your mind.

This way no one wins.

Oh, wait I forgot you are friends with Parkinson's.

Well, this isn't the end my old foe.

I still have a long way to go.

My new BMW

When I was working full time before I received my Parkinson Diagnosis and things began to change, I eventually had to stop working although still managing to volunteer with a disabled organisation.

My old mode of transport would have been a new company car every 3 years and my new mode of transport is now a 4mh electric wheelchair.

Which did I enjoy most? Perhaps I won't go down that road but please don't feel sorry for me I have learned so much about myself and how to adjust and take things at a much slower pace I can travel the one mile to my local shops and in that time have 3 or 4 conversations with strangers I meet in the street.

I can improve someone's day and notice if they are struggling, I am in no rush to get anywhere anymore a simple wave a hello and you can be on your way.

A huge benefit is my appreciation of nature and even the changes in the weather you become much more in tune and at a pace which allows you to enjoy the simple things in life ok apart from the 140 bus!!! But the others are ok.

It really is about adjusting my mindset to what is now as opposed to what has gone, did I say it was easy well if I did that would be a complete lie, no it has been challenging but I am learning more about myself all the time and I am enjoying the experience, am I a martyr to the cause? Absolutely not but we move forward, or we stop altogether and when was that ever the answer.

Your body just won't work.

Parkinson's when your legs won't work.

When your feet get stuck.

When your muscles are tight.

You can't sleep at night.

Fatigue feels it's the worst it's been.

It's so hard to just not give in.

You just must ride the storm.

And pray that things improve in the morn.

Will I ever sleep again.

Night turns into day.

I wish sleep would get in the way.

But it refuses to be involved in the debate.

Even if I stay up late.

Whatever I do makes no difference to you.

I just must accept my fate.

Raining cats and dogs.

Wheelchair life

It's raining cats and dogs.

Wheelchair life is no fun.

Especially in the heavy rain.

How I long for some sun.

Waterproof jacket can I get my money back.

Soaked through I expect to see Noah.

Floating past in his ark.

Wheelchair life is no fun.

How I wish I could still run.

Freezing of Gait.

A symptom of Parkinson's Disease that is a big issue for me.

Manifests in a complete stop or prolonged shuffle in the feet or legs despite my best efforts and intention to move forward.

No medication or surgery are currently available to treat it.

Greatly increasing my risk of falling.

Electric Wheelchair.

I think everyone should have to use a wheelchair.

Manual or electric just for a day.

Then they might listen to what we say

Planning a journey.

Wheelchair life when your world gets smaller.

And your friends get fewer.

Everything you do everywhere you go.

It requires the type of military planning.

That might be required for a visiting head of state.

Is he still going on about wheel-chairs.

What shops will I visit today.

Ah but do they have a step that would get in the way.

Do they have a lift to the second floor.

Will my wheelchair go through the door.

Who put all these display stands covering the shop floor.

On a good day I imagine I am dodging in and

out the bollards in my new sports car.

But on a bad day I end up knocking them over, contents scattering near and far.

Parkinson's really is no fun.

Hallucinations. Delusions. Memory loss. Apathy. Depression. Anxiety.

Rigidity. Pain. Can't Sleep. Constipation. Choking. Freezing/ Falls.

Slurred Speech. Cramping. Tremor. Mobility.

Some of the joys of Parkinson's Disease.

Making the most of Parkinson's

Parkinson's Disease

The legs won't work.

The pain is unseen.

But it travels through the body.

At lightning speed.

You don't sleep so it can't be a dream.

More meds will be what you need.

What else can they do when they look at you.

They don't have a cure.

Your options are fewer.

Make the best but it's hard to rest.

It's Parkinson's Disease.

Wheelchair life in a strange town.

I had a fantastic holiday with my grown-up kids who look out for me.

I am accustomed to my powered chair in my own environment, that can be daunting enough but in a strange town.

I learned that drop kerbs are a problem everywhere also uneven payments so dangerous.

Some cafés and shops are wheelchair friendly others not so much, pretty much the same experience as at home.

Open air markets now that can be a challenge spending an hour looking at people's backsides, and in a crowded environment they suddenly stop without warning,

Not my fault you have sore ankles.

Thank God not many people smoke anymore so you are not dodging lit cigarettes.

Cobbled streets that bounce you around, will that car stop or wont he.

Most people don't mean to be a problem they are just unaware of your needs.

When they are aware they are usually happy to help.

I had a great time in Stratford upon Avon aka Shakespeare Country.

Parkinson's Disease, compulsive behaviour.

One of the biggest problems the disease brings is impulsive compulsive behaviour.

That could be spending money on things that you don't need.

It could be excessive gambling.

It could be excessive use of alcohol.

It could be sex.

It could be eating disorders.

Quite literally anything, but it is a horrible part of Parkinson's and medication that is poorly understood and rarely talked about.

Perhaps a lack of knowledge or embarrassment.

Awareness and understanding the patient is the key to helping them.

Happiness.

Happiness is when you realise its morning and you feel reasonably ok and haven't been awake half the night, you haven't had leg cramps and your Rem was under control.

Do I still need this hospital bed with the sides on like a cot.

Parkinson's Dementia.

In the later stages of Parkinson's Disease.

Some people will develop cognitive changes.

That ultimately lead to dementia and some people can.

Exhibit reactive behaviours, usually involving anxiety, anger.

And aggression.

This can include verbal outbursts such as shouting, swearing, or name calling.

Picking up the pieces.

Parkinson's Disease Dementia

When your brain does things, it shouldn't do.

And your mouth says things it shouldn't say.

And you must pick up the pieces the following day.

It's just the way.

It took another turn today.

My Dementia took another turn today.

It was a strange feeling like I knew what I was doing.

But it seemed to be happening in slow motion.

I was in a café and just exiting the disabled toilet.

I saw the back of a man standing a few yards in front of me.

He had his back to me, not causing me any harm.

For some unbelievable reason I went to pay the lady for my coffee.

I could hear his voice and a rush of anger went right through my body.

And I deliberately crashed into the back of his legs with my wheelchair.

I left without giving an apology quite proud of myself.

Of course, I did the correct thing today and reached out to him.

I apologised profusely and thankfully he accepted without argument.

What is going on with me.

Just another Parkinson day.

The cramp the pain.

It's so hard to explain.

Will it ever go away.

Or sadly is it here to stay.

The legs won't work.

Your feet are stuck.

It's not ok.

its going to be a long day.

Your hands to sore to open the door.

Look out the window the sky is grey.

I'm not going out anyway.

Night Cramping.

Parkinson's = Cramp

Parkinson's = Cramp

Parkinson's = Cramp

Parkinson's = Cramp

New Electric Wheelchair.

First time on the bus in my new wheelchair.

Driver was lovely and very helpful.

As were the dozen passenger's seated downstairs.

Got stuck twice which was not too bad.

I appreciate now that size does indeed matter.

I will get used to the extra power and manoeuvring with a touch.

Practice makes perfect and breeds confidence.

I can do this.

More than you see.

Parkinson's so much more than you see.

Once it gets a grip you can't get free.

It can change who you are.

Who you wanted to be.

The future is unclear.

As people disappear.

Life Observations/
Motivational

People Watching.

It's raining outside as I sit on my own.

Have my coffee in hand as I watch people come and go about their day.

I am in a café in a large shop invisible to most people watching what they are doing and listening to what they say.

Young and old they pass me by.

Some with a sparkle and some with a tear in their eye

We are all the same we all have a story to tell.

I wish I could listen to everyone.

and hear their story.

Find out the truth behind the eyes.

I sit I smile I nod and now and then I ask someone if they are well.

That is my morning until my friends arrive.

Respond don't react.

Respond don't react.

Words can hurt for a lifetime.

You can't take them back.

Think before you speak.

Stranger on the bus

Who is he where does she come from.

I am trying to decide are they happy or sad.

We all have one thing in common we are all on the same bus at the same time.

Each with our own thoughts.

People reading a magazine looking out the window or more likely to be on their mobile phones.

Not many people look happy.

Not many people conversing.

If one says hello does that make one a weir-do.

Youngsters old people, it's my stop soon.

I may as well have had the bus to myself.

I feel a sense of sadness although I did say good morning to everyone I met.

Some smiled back some held their heads low.

But that's ok smiling and saying hello is a start.

Hopefully it catches on.

Right the sun is out its time to sit in the park.

Enjoy time on your own.

It is amazing what you can achieve on your own.

Be who you want to be.

Live your own life.

Do things in your own time.

Enjoy the space and quiet.

The 140-bus saga continues.

Well, it is cold today the footpaths are covered in ice.

I had no choice I had to get the dreaded 140

bus.

Not been on it for a while so it took me a couple of attempts at reversing my wheelchair into the ridiculously tight space.

The bus was quiet for a change, and I had a lovely chat with an elderly gentleman and a very nice lady, all going well I thought.

Then the bust pulled into my stop, the driver had apparently mis judged the distance from the bus to the kerbside.

That left the problem that he could not lower his ramp which would allow me to leave the bus.

I spent the next 10 minutes, or it seemed that long, being manoeuvred pushed and pulled before I along with my wheelchair were man-handled from the bus.

To make matters worse there was about a dozen people waiting to get on the bus.

Dignity and feel-good factor disappeared in these 10 minutes; Embarrassment took over.

To the driver's credit he also felt bad and kept apologising to me, which I appreciated and once off the bus I reset myself and thought this won't ruin my day.

Just part of everyday life when you must use a wheelchair.

Derelict building

I always feel a mixture of sad and curious.

When I see a derelict house or factory.

At one time these places were full of people going about their lives

Perhaps generations of families lived in the houses.

As for the factories one can only speculate as to how many people worked within these walls and what stories they could tell of lives now passed.

Have you ever stood outside a house that you and your family once lived in and just closed your eyes, and the memories came flooding back.

Yes, me too.

Mrs Doyle.

For those of you who have watched the television show Father Ted on TV imagine the character Mrs Doyle, for those of you who are unfamiliar with the character imagine two middle aged ladies sitting together gossiping enjoy pots of tea and plates of sandwiches.

Lady 1   I am really tired I only get 4 hours sleep a night.

Lady 2   Really well I only get 3 hours sleep a night.

Lady 1   I get tired about 3pm and perhaps have a short nap.

Lady 2   Oh I get tired, but I never have a nap in the day.

Lady 1   I have baked biscuits for the church sale.

Lady 2   Oh I have baked biscuits but also made a chocolate cake for the church sale.

The conversation goes on but hopefully by now you get the idea it was so funny to listen to and witness.

To be fair I have no idea how they heard each other as neither seemed to stop talking long enough to draw breath.

Don't you just love people, oh and I often wondered who paid the bill.

Need for coffee.

It is inhumane in my opinion.

To force people who genuinely have a medi-cal need for coffee.

To have to wait in line behind people who apparently view the act as some kind of rec-reational activity.

What are pavements for?

Walking. Wheelchairs. Pushchairs. Prams.

What are they not for.

Cars. Vans. Supermarket trollies.

Wheelie Bins. Mattresses. Dog Poo.

I could go on, but you get my point.

Just another hurdle to life in a wheelchair.

Invisible

Have you ever felt invisible.

Even in a crowded room.

It's like everyone is having real life fun.

And your left watching on zoom.

You speak but nobody hears.

You wave but nobody looks.

It's like you are the only person in the room.

Spring in the air.

You can almost smell spring in the air.

It's still quite cold but at least its fare.

Looking forward to long light nights.

Sun hot in the sky shining bright.

Winter clothes will be packed away.

Shirts and shorts the order of the day.

I am sure my shirts have shrunk.

While waiting on the sun.

Nothing to do with comfort eating and scoffing chocolate buns.

Anyway, we still have a few months to wait.

The summertime, the light nights the warm days.

Make me feel great.

The thought of spring

I love the thought of springtime.

New life new hope longer nights.

I never get tired wondering at the beauty of nature.

Life whether it be that of a plant pushing up through the soil.

Or the cries of a new-born baby.

Life in all its glory

It really is a wondrous story.

Americano

McDonalds americano early on a Friday morning

Quiet and peaceful, and coffee much nicer than

The major coffee shops.

Perfect start to the weekend.

What's not to like.

Bus journey home

When you're on the bus home

Its dark outside the bus is cold.

The father and son sitting in front of me.

Are watching rugby on their phone.

With full commentary.

Man, then gets on the bus with his mobile phone on speaker.

Promising his undying love for whoever is unfortunate enough to be on the other end of the phone, oh! And what time he will be home for his dinner.

Some might think he had something to hide, but I am surely not that judgemental.

But I do wish I owned a time machine.

Did I mention the lady slurping loudly on her can of cheap cola drink.

Anyway, soon be home.

Happy Tuesday

I have a meeting at lunchtime.

But as usual I am an hour early.

Which you will know by now I prefer.

People I meet seem happier this morning.

And I am trying to work out why that would be.

I take a seat; I order a large Americano as usual.

Read my book that I have just bought called Jesus and the Essenes.

It is fascinating but my mind doesn't seem to be taking in the information.

But I will persevere as the author Dolores Cannon fascinates me.

I was already in a cheery mood when I checked to see if anyone had left a review.

On my own publication 'what if by Graham Thomson'

And the answer is an emphatic yes.

Another review

Thank you.

Don't be so angry.

2023 I look around and I watch and listen I read stories in local newspapers.

The one thing that strikes me is never have people owned as many material possessions but here is the question why people are still so angry, what is making them mad.

I guess all the material goods in the world won't make a sad man glad.

Happiness is not found in things it is found in people.

Don't be angry or mad try to make someone's day happy, be kind be patient.

say good morning think before you judge it is the best feeling in the world knowing people

are happier for having known you even in a small way.

Be the difference kindness is contagious, pass it on.

The Time Machine.

Have you ever wondered how you got to a certain point in your life.

What would you say the turning point was.

If given a second chance, would you make the same choices.

Would you do things differently.

Perhaps you would follow the same path.

Then again with the gift of hindsight you might make changes.

The truth is we can't go back, and we make the most of what we have and where we are.

We live the best life we can with optimism love and gratitude at the forefront.

Life is a blessing but don't forget to also bless others.

Life is too short to hold grudges or hang onto resentment.

Is he spying on me.

Yes, he is on my bus again.

Do you think he is spying on me.

Absolutely, or am I just unlucky.

He seems to be aware of when I get the bus.

Even when I change my times.

He doesn't look like Mi5 but then again.

What does an Mi5 agent look like.

Hmmm it makes you wonder.

I love my hats.

I have a hat for every day of the week.

I think I look suave I think I look sleek.

Fedora, flat cap, wide rimmed Panama.

Gives style and makes me stand out from the
crowd.

Straw, cotton or leather I really don't care.

As I walk on past people usually stare.

I guess it's unusual to see a man with such flare.

I love my hats.

Mixed up letters.

Writing poetry can help to clear your mind.

But not always.

Sometimes it's just jumbled up letters that make no sense.

British Summer Time.

Lighter nights, welcome to the official start of British Summer Time (BST)

What that means in practice remains to be seen

In my mind lots if sunshine and warm evenings.

Nice long drives in my wheelchair.

A couple of holidays thrown in would be nice.

But they would require precise planning.

The reality is probably damp days with heavy rain.

And precious little sun.

Let's hope it's not the second one.

Most of us function better and feel happier.

When the sun shines.

I pray that the sun shines on you.

Monday Morning.

140 bus this morning its freezing cold.

Forced to listen to a blow-by-blow account of.

The Scotland game on Saturday and how we must

Surely be contenders to win the next world cup.

Although no expansion was given on the thought

Process of the previous statement.

Get to Morrisons café and only 3 young ladies in the

Queue in front of me, then I hear the dreaded words.

Can we have 6 build your own breakfasts please.

6 I'm thinking that's strange, then I notice a child attached to

Each mother.

On the plus side if you want to know the price of bacon sausages beans in Morrisons Café

Then I'm your man, on the downside I might not live long enough to give you the answer.

Have a happy Monday wherever you are.

Spread the love.

If I could give any advice, it would be this.

Surround yourself with positive people.

Avoid judgemental bitter angry negative people.

Please don't listen to the gossips.

Treat others as you find them and try to be a positive influence.

Within your community within your family

circle and friends.

Be the difference and spread love do not hate.

Men and sport.

What turns mild mannered granddads and well brought up teenagers?

Men of all ages, status, and ethnic origin.

Into raving lunatics when they go to a football match any level of football.

That makes no difference to the mindset.

Shouting, swearing, giving verbal abuse and in some instances physical abuse.

Faces grimacing in hate toward the opposition.

When similar men from the same town from the same schools.

Can watch other sports and yes, consuming the same amount of alcohol.

Yet behave in a totally acceptable way, with an attitude of enjoying their day.

Everyone has a story.

Everyone has a story.

We all have a tale to tell.

We only see what we want to see.

You must guess the rest.

Saturday morning the lady with the bruise on her face

And she said she fell.

But she looks ill at ease is something wrong?

I just can't tell.

We all have shadows we get good at hiding them away.

But don't be afraid to ask for help.

It really is ok.

Stronger than you think.

You're stronger than you think.

You can achieve more than you know.

Trust yourself and let your feelings show.

Don't be scared don't run away.

Stand tall chest out you smashed it today.

You can do this be proud of who you are.

Cast your doubts and worries away.

And lock them in a jar.

Life in 23 for me.

Life in 23 for me.

Scan bar codes for this.

QR codes for that.

I just want a waitress to stop and chat.

Technology moves to fast for me, I just can't express.

If I had to sit an exam, I would probably be last.

Hopefully that's not true as I would do my best.

I might just scrape a pass.

If I sat that test.

Or I could just do what I usually do and phone my children.

Easter weekend.

Easter weekend in the sun.

With your favourites is so much fun.

The banter the laughs in the city of the bard.

Shakespeare or the Parkie Poet.

Surely the decision is not hard.

You Decide.

You get to decide.

You get to choose.

Whatever you decide.

You have nothing to lose.

Your life your way.

You get the final say.

The park bench and me.

The park is quiet just me and the statue in
memory of the heroes who served and sadly.

Gave their lives for Queen and country.

A nice breeze blows although a bit cold.

That's how I like it.

I'm getting old.

The fresh air is good for my mental health.

The air we breathe is free, regardless of wealth.

I embrace nature at its best.

The dog sitting watching me, the cat sitting watching the dog.

The moment has gone.

It didn't last long.

Long enough to lift my brain fog.

It's coffee time it calls my name.

Geniuses of the day.

Marc Bolan and Bob Dylan

Two men who were craftsmen.

Artists in every way.

Poets and writers very much of their day.

They could tell a story with passion and fire.

Love passion and war.

I would never tire.

Originals talented geniuses of their day,

When they had nothing to work with.

They found a way.

Marc taken too you not yet reached his prime.

But his music lives on in the eternity of time.

Lonely.

Being alone doesn't make you lonely.

Being with the wrong people does.

Living in a bubble.

Did you get your new I Phone? OMG the camera is so much better on the new one.

My new laptop is so light I can lift it with just 2 fingers.

Did you see our neighbour's brand new car, lucky sod.

I do need a new I Phone to be fair, mine is

almost a year old.

What was that you said about the collapsed mine in the Congo.

Where is that? What, hundreds of people buried alive aw that's a shame.

What? No, I don't know anything about how many children are starving in the world.

Or natural disasters leaving millions home-less, I can't be expected to know everything.

I know it's sad eh!! Oh, I was just saying the Samsung camera isn't as good as the I Phone.

Listen don't start on me I give £1.00 per week to cancer research; I do my bit.

Live in a bubble, me!!! How dare you.

With Respect.

I am not bothered where you shop.

Or that your delivery comes today.

Indeed, what your mother has to say.

It's very nice that your partner loves you.

I got it the 3rd time I heard you say.

If you look at me and start talking, I assume you're talking to me.

I didn't see the earphone thing sticking through your long hair, is this 1983?

20 people on the bus and 16 of them were on their mobile phones.

All I can hear is a massive drone.

The biggest addiction in the world is the mobile phone.

Coffee is love.

If you love somebody

Let them go.

If they come back with Coffee.

It was meant to be.

Sometimes I'm glad to be single.

Husband spends £400.00 per month on video games.

Wife watches Netflix and plays online bingo every night.

They go out individually with friends at the weekend.

Between them they are £25.000 in debt.

Which does not include their mortgage.

8 credit cards between them, mostly maxed out.

They hardly communicate with each other.

Thank Goodness I am single.

It got up and went.

If anyone finds my get up and go.

Could you please send it back to me.

First class or recorded delivery please.

I really need it for tomorrow.

If I was a tree.

If I was a tree

What would I see.

Who planted me.

If I could talk, what would I tell.

What secrets could I unveil.

All four seasons they come and go.

If I had a preference, it would be the snow.

Generations come and go.

Secrets are safe with me.

All the knowledge that I know.

Will never leave me.

Signed the tree.

Hospital is full.

How many people are in hospital because of addiction.

How many because of mental health.

Not a judgement, just an observation.

When you add on the amount of people

Who can go home but are waiting on a care package.

 which can take months.

You see where part of the problem lies.

Do you remember in the UK the home helps.

I don't think it was appreciated just what a valuable

Job, they did for society.

The dating App.

The dating app game.

Where each has no name.

Have they told the truth.

How old is that picture in the frame.

I think you might need proof.

Is anything real.

Not much you feel.

You can do it.

You can do it.

How do you know?

Because I know who you are.

Is that so.

How can you know from afar.

Because I know you.

Well, I hope you are right.

I really do.

My first public show.

My first public show.

How will it go.

All the tickets have been sold.

40 will attend.

A mixture of ages young and old.

Thank you for bringing a friend.

When I said sold.

That's not strictly true.

The tickets are free.

From me to you.

Pour a coffee, take a seat.

And please enjoy the show.

Keep women safe.

Every two or three days in the UK, a female is dead as a result of the actions of a male.

What society do we live in where half of the population live in fear from the other half.

These figures do not include domestic violence or abuse emotional or sexual.

It makes me ashamed, and I wonder what can be done to make women free safer.

Decent men are scared to speak to women they don't know, and women are fearful or at least unsure and wary of speaking to men.

Broken Britain.

Live your best life.

Don't be bitter.

Don't be mad.

Don't be vengeful.

Don't be sad.

Don't live in the past.

Don't dwell on what's gone.

Don't forget, the pain won't last.

Live your best life now.

Be kind to yourself.

Be kind to yourself.

Stop picking fault.

Focus on the good you do.

Work on your inner self.

That is where you will find your wealth.

Try to be honest and true.

All the good work begins with you.

You are the author of your life.

Don't be angry they say.

Don't be bitter they say.

What is done is done they say.

You can't change the past they say.

You must look to the future they say.

And they are 100% correct.

You can't change the past only learn from it.

Don't give it airtime in your head.

Live your best life now and in the future.

You are the author, your autobiography.

You decide.

Religious/Spiritual

Sue me.

Jehovah's Witnesses and other cult religions ruin people lives.

Beware of smiling faces proclaiming the truth.

Insisting only, they have the knowledge they have the proof.

What they won't tell you is the doctrine they preach is based on lies.

They all live while everyone else dies.

Please take my advice and stay well clear.

They run their religion based on fear.

The easiest thing is to stay well clear.

Tomorrow

Don't be scared to let your emotions show.

It's the only way your soul can grow.

Don't supress your feelings.

If it makes you feel better.

Let the tears flow.

Remember tomorrow is a new day.

One God

One God so many religions.

So much conflict.

So many wars.

Leaders with giant crosses draped around their necks.

And wearing pantomime gowns.

Storing their wealth while telling us how we should live.

Why don't we just cut out the middleman and just pray.

God is everywhere.

God is everywhere.

God is everything.

God is beyond our imagination.

God cannot be worked out.

God cannot be blamed.

God does not need to be worshiped.

God is not religion.

God does not need to be understood.

God is eternal as is our soul.

God is love.

God is part of you in this life and beyond.

God has this.

When you look around at the state of the world

The anger and the greed

To fear the outcome

There is no need.

Have faith God has got this.

Talk with God

Close your eyes and talk to God.

Call it prayer if you prefer.

The name doesn't matter.

Just believe that he is there.

Say what you think.

Say what you feel.

You won't hurt his feelings.

So just keep it real.

Religion and the Church

Religion and the church are man-made institutions created to control and suppress the mass population and make those people at the top very wealthy.

Spirituality is a one-to-one relationship with your creator without the drama or guilt.

You're a sinner.

You're a sinner.

How can you be so bad.

We should trust our churches more.

You know the people that hand round a begging bowl every Sunday because as we all know they are so poor.

Not starving poor, you understand maybe just can't afford to replace the state-of-the-art music system.

Or the ornate stain glass windows with just toughened glass.

Most don't pay tax either.

But at least they use the money for good e.g., help the poor feed the hungry home the homeless? Don't they? or do they invest the money in more property and concentrate on the material things they don't want you or me to have, and just go through the motions regarding the needy.

I don't remember reading about Jesus selling tickets for the sermon on the mount or charging people for individual miracles.

God is free and always will be.

Jehovah Witnesses.

Jehovah Witnesses.

Cult Religion.

Cover up Child Abuse.

Cover up domestic abuse.

Organisations corrupt to the core.

accept the Watchtower and Awake your life

will never be the same again.

Don't do it.

The end of the world.

Imagine you were told the world was going to end in a particular year.

Would that fill you with fear.

What would you do, imagine again that you had given up on your Education your career getting married having children, even giving your money away.

What would you say.

When that year came and went without incident, how would you feel regarding the organisation that had convinced you.

You had given up everything for them.

They didn't apologise back then instead they are still perpetuating the myth and the lie 47 years later and people are still buying into the lies and deceit.

Why seriously just why.

Cult life the question is why.

Why do sensible people follow cults.

What makes them believe what seems like the unbelievable.

What are they searching for? Could it be the meaning of life.

Could it be they feel the need to belong in some way?

I often ask myself that question without finding the answers that make sense to me.

They hear voices from somewhere, in extreme cases resulting in mass suicide.

Some people spend their lives searching and arguing who is right and who is wrong.

Which book to believe if any.

Instead of enjoying the life they have making kindness and love the priority.

Trusting in the creator that whatever happens next will turn out fine.

As Paul McCartney once said.

All you need is love.

What do you say in prayer.

When you need more inner strength.

Where does it come from.

How do you do it.

What motivates you to keep going.

If you pray, what do you say.

Is it God the creator or the source.

Perhaps your higher self.

Whatever gets you through the day.

You must put in the work.

There is no easy way.

Spring clean

They live rent free.

In the vacuum of your mind.

You think they care how much space the take up.

Cleanse your mind and throw them out.

It's time to have a spring clear out.

If it doesn't serve you or make you feel good.

If it constantly worries, you or lowers your mood.

Pray to God and hear him say.

My child put your worries in a balloon.

And watch them fly away.

Trust in God each time you pray.

Just Pray.

When you're worried, pray.

When you're anxious, pray.

When you're thankful, pray.

When you're not sure who you are praying to, pray.

When you need strength, pray.

When you're ill, pray.

When you're healthy, pray.

When you're confused, pray.

When you love life, pray.

In fact, just pray.

God and Nature.

Beautiful spring day.

Summer is on the way.

Gardens blooming in colour.

I intend to enjoy every single day.

Nature is God's way.

No words are required to say.

I love you.

Don't give up.

Having a rough day.

Place your hand on your heart.

Do you feel that.

That's called purpose,

You're alive for a reason.

Don't give up.

You survived.

Did it happen should it matter.

What happens if you look back.

Do you turn to stone.

As you walk away alone.

Can you find your way home.

Or will you come under attack.

For daring to fight back.

Only time will tell.

If you survived and it ended well

A walk in the woods.

Walking through the quiet woods' tears in my eyes.

After what they did to me it's no surprise.

Time heals and then out from the blue.

The feelings you had so long ago.

Rush back to you.

Nothing you can do or say.

Can ever take the pain away.

Maybe one day they will be made to pay.

Obsessed.

Why are many religions obsessed with the end of the world and believe the God they profess to love will take great pleasure in wiping out most people on earth.

When will they realise that God is love and have that spiritual awakening and realise that no Armageddon is coming, God lives in each of us.

Spirituality not religion.

Message from God.

Never trust a person who says they have received a message from God.

That could have been meant for half the country.

Poor God gets the blame for everything.

Also never trust anyone who need to write out 2 pages of prayers.

If it does not come from your heart, it means
nothing.

But it's in the bible.

Whenever Christians say, but it's biblical?

I get uneasy, smashing an enemy's infant
against a rock.

That's biblical.

I'm much more interested in if it's Christ like.

Political

Enough is enough.

Politicians hoarding money in offshore bank accounts.

Shareholders and CEOs receiving pay-outs from companies that are losing money.

Large companies trading and making millions of pounds here in the UK but paying tax elsewhere.

Governments hoarding money for their own political agenda without proper audits being carried out.

While people who are working must go to food banks and charity shops to make ends meet.

Disabled people who are prisoners in their own homes because their local bus service has been withdrawn and subsidised taxi cabs funding stopped.

Is this the Britain we want in 2023 it is time to start making Governments accountable in whatever form that takes.

Enough is surely enough it's time to fight back and make fairness the truth and the way forward.

The rich get richer.

At what point do everyday people stand up and unite and say no more.

The rich get richer as they throw the everyday man in the street a small crumb from their wealthy table.

They don't care about the massed population.

It's not like they have ever had to use public transport or have set foot in a library perish the thought they might have had to use a public loo.

They create more wealth for the few.

At the expense of people like me and you.

While morale in our emergency services is at an all-time low.

Working people use food banks to make ends meet.

More homeless people living on the street.

The corruption and deceit from all our governments continue to grow.

When will the time come when the people rise and shout NO.

We have had and seen enough.

You Decide

Just another Politician lining his own pocket while the rest of us pay.

This is not just a UK problem but an issue worldwide.

Never have we faced such a worldwide epidemic of Politicians.

Who shall we say are at best economical with the truth.

Even when the evidence is clear and the and we have the proof.

Nothing changes as they are all members of the same money-making club.

To which the rest of the population are not allowed to join.

They lie and they sneer when we dare to ask questions, they continue to remain aloof.

It is a scandal they are not being held to account for their behaviour and lack of respect.

For the average person in the street.

It appears to me we all feel the same at least the people I speak to and meet.

So, what do we do who do we trust.

The answer is somewhere and find it we must.

Political Party

Political party I have none.

However, I do believe we are stronger as one.

Fairness for all.

A fair day's wage whatever your age.

Vulnerable disabled and elderly.

Respected and looked after.

Real job with prospects security offered.

Better education available to all.

NHS run efficiently funded properly.

Available to all at the point of call.

Hard work the ethos without the greed.

This is the only way that we will succeed.

Opinions are banned.

We live in a world where opinions are banned.

The situation will only get worse.

Unless we all take a stand.

Freedom of speech in a civilised world.

Should be a right for all that we understand.

The right to agree to disagree seems to have been lost.

To debate with each other without hate.

We must protect our liberty and rights at all costs.

A world that won't learn.

60 years ago, when I was aged 3, nuclear war was avoided at the last moment.

Using diplomacy. But the Americans would have you believe it was their show of force that saved the day, they can have it their own way.

Here we are again back in a similar position with Biden forcing Putin into a corner and we all know what happens when people think have only one option to save face.

Millions of people are dying in the Ukraine which has been horrible for those involved and those people watching helplessly.

But in a nuclear war situation what is happening in Ukraine would be a mere drop in the ocean.

Are we ok with that? Are we willing to sit back and let the two most powerful men in the world destroy everything and everyone.

For what exactly, nobody can win the Ukraine war.

It seems to me we are back where we were in 1963 where someone might claim a victory which it won't be, we all know the only way to peace is through talking and diplomacy which must prevail and the irresponsible rhetoric from both sides must stop now before it's too late.

What has happened to the world?

I ask myself that question every day.

More greed, more corruption, by governments of the world.

We surely must find a better way.

It's like we have learned nothing over the thousands of years of civilisation.

Or maybe that's not quite true.

Because there is plenty for the many, but the wealth is controlled by the few.

They hold onto what they have with all their might.

Feed the hungry help the needy help countries and people sustain themselves.

Wait a minute what is in it for us, that will be right.

They will just keep telling lies they think we don't understand.

What they will do and their master plan, just keep voting for me it will be alright.

Well, that is a lie as sure as day follows night.

If there is a greater power, watching looking at the greed the hypocrisy and the mass corruption.

Now would be a good time to join the fight.

So, we can live in a world with justice for all,

With fairness and honesty or the Governments fall.

House of cards

It collapses like a house of cards.

Who thought it was ok to have husband and wife?

Having control of a country.

Millions missing will they ever be found.

Are they in foreign banks or a hole in the

ground.

Will the truth be told; will they end up in jail.

Will the rule of law and justice prevail.

Corrupt to the core telling us what we need.

While stealing more money their fat mouths they must feed.

The cars go back the house and the camper-van sold.

When they get out of jail.

I hope they are very old.

Big brother watching you.

They hear all and they see everything we do.

In 2023 big brother is watching everything you do.

From the cameras that record your every move.

Our mobile phones tell them where you have been.

Who you have spoken with.

Even if not seen your electronic footprint reveals history.

About your life you might or might not want

people to know.

Public platforms contain information clearly on show.

You never think as you fill it with information about where you go.

Your life is public whether to the government who can track your phone.

Or follow you on camera.

Or on social media where you volunteer your work what you like to eat.

And even your home.

Are you single are you married its not hard to find out.

Where your kids go to school and what time they come out.

We should be more careful what we freely give away.

Who liked what or how many comments you check each day.

A bit more privacy is a better way.

Big brother is already monitoring your every move.

They would deny it of course and insist its for our safety.

What else would you expect them to say.

Relationships

I gave you, my heart.

She was a friend a very good friend.

That's a very good place to start.

It was only a matter of time you say.

Before she stole your heart.

What would you do.

If you were in a marriage that was ok.

I mean not great but ok.

Whether for one year or forty years.

And despite trying and talking things just didn't change.

What would you do what would your decision depend on.

Would you reluctantly settle for projecting a lie to the outside world.

Or would you say life is too short and we both deserve to be happy.

The sad thing is statistics show that conversation hardly ever takes place.

Between bored and unsettled couples.

What would you do.

You can do it on your own.

Because they text you last thing at night and first thing in the morning doesn't mean you were their last and first thought.

Don't be fooled with words especially through the smell of alcohol.

Judge people on how they treat you not what they say to you or what they buy you.

Someone who takes time to listen to what you have to say.

They care about your opinion they may not always agree but love you anyway.

Be with someone who helps you through the sad times as well as enjoying the good times.

And if you haven't found that person then that's ok.

Be happy and content with who you are and enjoy life your own way.

Life is a wonderful adventure don't waste it on someone who didn't deserve it.

It is your life go out and live it.

Fly free.

You don't have to be part of a wee.

You can do it on your own.

Life changes with us.

As we get older, we change and life changes with us it must develop and grow.

People will come and go.

And that is not always a bad thing.

Different friends bring new ideas and help us in unique ways.

We can give love and retrieve love many times over.

It can take many forms.

Love and respect yourself.

Don't be afraid to set boundaries be happy and content with who you are.

Never settle for second best.

Why?

Why do we feel the need to belong?

and when you turn on the radio

what will be the most played song.

Love and heartache where did I go wrong.

We don't need to search for another half.

To help us reach our goal.

You are already whole this is your story you are the author, and you decide your goal.

Ora meaning light in Hebrew.

Little Ora so small so sweet

Not yet big enough to fill a seat.

But she is blessed to have such a warm kind mum.

Her blonde hair glistens in the morning sun.

Her energy and kindness for all to see.

I am very happy she spoke to me.

Not all bus Journeys are bad.

Two old men.

Two old guys sitting in a café.

One is drinking coffee.

And the other a pot of tea.

The older man is my friend Davie.

And the younger man is me.

Today we are grumpy old men.

And complain about everything we see.

Apart from my black coffee.

And his delicious pot of tea

The power of song.

The pain of a loved one long since gone.

But memories stirred by a single song.

Your heart takes you back to a long-lost place.

Where you wish you had a chance to say to their face.

I love you I miss you I try to be strong.

I still can't believe that you are gone.

Divorce.

What does it mean.

How are you meant to feel.

Do you have to stop loving the person.

Is that what it takes to make it real.

What happens if you can't do that.

What is left. Where do you go.

Is there a book that has been written.

To explain in detail how you are meant to feel.

The reason I ask is a selfish one.

Because as of today I am single again.

I don't know if it feels real.

And I certainly don't know how I feel.

Broken Heart.

My heart it breaks.

My soul it aches.

Time spent on my own.

Watching TV.

Or scrolling through my phone.

What Now.

My mind is blank.

My memories gone.

I feel so week.

When I need to be strong.

Workmates.

Do people you work with count as friends.

If you were to leave your job tomorrow.

In say one year's time.

How many if any.

Would still be in your life.

You Got This.

Don't let them win.

They have taken enough.

You have been strong.

You have been tough.

They will pay for the sin.

After all these years.

You would be mad to let them win.

You can do this.

You did it before.

You can do it again.

With the help of family and friends.

You got this.

Malt Whisky.

You are like a single malt whisky.

Just one taste is perfection.

But drinking the whole bottle.

Will surely kill me.

Family at Easter

What a wonderful easter weekend

Away with my two favourites.

I am blessed to have such kind caring children.

Who look after the old man and organise things.

To make sure I am ok.

I am truly grateful and blessed.

Thank you both and love you millions.

You made every day good.

You made my day.

You lift me with your smile.

When u felt low you would pick me up.

Without even knowing because that's just who you are.

Serving my coffee in a takeaway cup.

Always with a smile taking time to chat.

I will always be grateful to you for that.

No more smiley faces on my coffee cup.

You move onto a fresh challenge.

And your career begins for real.

I will always be grateful for the way you made me feel.

Your family will be so proud of you.

You could do anything you choose.

But don't change, keep smiling and you will never lose.

When you change your mind.

At least be brave enough to admit your choice.

Instead of pretending that you heard a voice.

God picked you out and he made it clear.

For your mental health from me you should steer.

People hear what they want to hear.

Poor God gets the blame for everything.

Meeting my niece in Costa.

Meeting my niece in costa

Very relaxing and enjoyable you think.

Meeting the family was truly lovely.

But the risking my life in the shopping centre car park

Not so much.

Cars are bigger and seem to be driven by people who have.

Difficulty in seeing over the bonnet.

No sense of awareness, yes red does mean stop.

No, you can't stop in the middle of a crossing.

When you reverse it's good to know nothing is behind you.

Best not to drive when you are looking at your phone.

Fun times, well it would be if it were not so dangerous.

I believe in angels.

When you are sitting in the park enjoying the fresh air.

Enjoying the flowers and the smell of a spring day.

Beautiful angel with two lovely dogs walks your way.

A lovely young lady with a story to tell.

Completely made my day.

I hope to see you soon.

You never lose it.

You never lose it.

I was on the bus coming home from the Hearts game.

The bus was very busy, but I managed to manoeuvre the

Wheelchair into the space.

The lady standing beside me liked my hat and I politely thanked her.

We get chatting and then she asked me out for a drink.

She also told me that she really liked my beard.

I thanked her but politely declined her offer.

Just like the old days.

Time Heals.

They say that time heals.

That's not the way it feels.

Do you talk to yourself.

Do your dreams seem real.

Can you see clear, that loved ones don't leave.

The emotions that you feel.

The touch the smell make you believe.

They are with you day and night.

Kissing you and holding you tight.

Why.

If someone keeps getting involved in arguments.

Perhaps they should as themselves why?

My Brother my best friend.

My brother my best friend.

All the good times we had.

We thought would never end.

The love and respect we shared.

I always knew you cared.

Big bro I thought we would go old.

As a team, as mates' life would be such fun.

I still remember the day we were told.

You were so calm, and I just wanted to run.

I still feel robbed after all these years.

And God knows I have cried a thousand

tears.

"a pint of special and a rum and black please."

Britain somewhere in the 70s.

They lived in a two up two down.

4 children sleeping in one room.

Dad worked in the shipyard during the week.

Mum looked after the 2 younger kids.

The older kids were on the dole.

Dad would get blind drunk every weekend.

Leaving mum to deal with the household chores.

And looking after the family.

Dad would be too quick to use his hands.

Every day seemed dark and bleak.

It didn't matter what day of the week.

This was their life on repeat.

The kids saw no hope ahead.

As they received another slap on the head.

They would pray to God and ask what the point is.

To be sure they would rather be dead.

Mind the door.

If you're leaving, when walking out the door please keep going.

Don't block the way for others waiting to come in.

Just half an hour.

When we lose a loved one.

The death often poses more questions than answers.

If we could just have half an hour with our loved one.

What questions would we ask.

Would half an hour be enough.

To discuss choices, they made

And make some sense of all the stuff'.

Things we have discovered about them since they died.

Confused us more as we mourn and cry.

Why did you do this, why did you do that.

What was the truth and what was a lie.

Did I really know you, things I never knew.

I don't think I ever really got to know the real you.

Special.

That person was never special.

It was your love that made them.

Special.

Well, that wasn't true.

She said she loved you.

Well, that wasn't true.

She said you were her soul mate.

Well, that wasn't true.

She said she would take care of you.

Well, that wasn't true.

She said she was proud of you.

Well, that wasn't true.

Was any of it true.

Between me and you.

Life Lessons/Quotes

Think outside the box.

Don't apologise for thinking outside the box.

Don't apologise for not conforming.

Don't apologise for living your own life.

Don't apologise for asking questions.

Don't apologise just be who you are.

This is your Gig do what you want.

You get to choose.

Hospital February 2023

Please forgive me if this makes no sense.

Liquid morphine has been my staple diet for the day.

I shouldn't complain it's my own fault I am in hospital this time.

I thought I could do what I couldn't.

Lesson learned without doubt.

Please God let me out.

As I write this will be my 15th hour in triage

Waiting to go to go to a ward it's like something you might see.

On the BBC

Except this is not TV, six inches between beds.

Patients cough and scream it's like a bad dream.

But of course, I'm awake how could you not be.

I came in here with soft tissue damage to my leg.

I feel like I'm dead and I have arrived in hell.

God if I survive tonight, I promise to repent.

I need more morphine why they won't give me more morphine.

My first published book.

Yesterday was such an exciting time for me.

My first book was published, and I felt I had achieved something.

I felt happy and relieved.

I love writing you see.

Even if it was just for me.

But to hold the book in my hand.

And read it through.

Brought back emotions both false and true.

I don't think I will ever come down from cloud nine.

What if by Graham Thomson aka the parkie poet is mine.

Oh, and yours if you go on Amazon.

Not my intention.

My writing and my poetry will not resonate with everyone.

That was never my intention.

However, if some of what I write resonates with you then great.

If not, I hope you non the less got something from the experience.

Remember the golden rule.

You are a fair person you are honest.

But hey we all like a bargain don't we.

We all like to think we can get a good deal.

But more and more people are trying to steal.

But there is no such thing as a free meal.

If it sounds too good to be true.

Remember the idea is to tempt you.

Remember the golden rule and don't be a fool.

Don't be tempted don't get conned.

If in doubt throw it out, delete the email.

Block your number on the phone.

Don't open the door and don't engage.

You work too hard for your money to give it away.

So, no matter what they say.

The answer is always NO.

The Ford Capri

Do you remember the ford capri, the bay city rollers, platform shoes, and trousers that stopped at the knee.

Jeez you must be as old as me.

TV with no remote control.

Recording the top 40 onto a TDK tape every Sunday, listening to the new charts on a Tuesday at school with your transistor radio stuck to your ear.

Top of the pops on a Thursday night with the gorgeous Pans People dancers.

The top twenty run down what would be number one.

Slade, T.REX or Terry Jacks seasons in the sun.

That song always made me cry, even to this day I don't know why.

The early to mid-70s long hair and attitude like we didn't care.

Smoking pot at the foot of the stair.

Gang fights on a Saturday night for those who had less class.

Me I was always more interested in finding a new lass.

The 70s the decade style forgot.

But as Pilot would say it was magic anyway.

Brave the shave.

I did brave the shave today.

Raising money for cancer research.

Thanks to my friend Renee.

Who shaved my thick black locks away.

Over £300 was raised by family and friends and staff from trust housing.

Honestly, we had such a laugh.

Talking about laughs and fun Denise took me to see her mum who is in a care home this afternoon, fill of mischief laughter and sticky buns.

I am however conscious that not everyone had a good day.

And I wish I could make their pain go away.

May God be with them in their journey.

Keep them safe from harm everyday lord this I pray.

Keep the dream alive.

Dreamers keep dreaming.

Believers keep believing.

Lovers keep loving.

Givers keep giving.

Explorers keep exploring.

Carers keep caring.

Travellers keep travelling.

Your life. You decide.

Don't let others derail your ride.

I Prefer the simple things.

I prefer peace and quiet to arguments and noise.

I prefer to meditate quietly than to over think.

I prefer relaxing with a mug of coffee as opposed to a cup of tea.

I prefer the quiet anticipation of the morning to the quiet loneliness of night.

I prefer to pray to God on a one to one as opposed to sitting in a church.

I prefer dark chocolate as opposed to milk chocolate.

I prefer a small circle of loyal friends as opposed to many acquaintances.

I prefer watching Football as opposed to rugby.

I prefer to eat ice cream of any kind when I am feeling low.

At my time of life.

I have been a professional person most of my life.

But you hit that age and your circumstances change.

Whether it be your health.

Maybe for the first time you can really be you.

No wife to impress.

No boss to fire you.

Hell, what are they all going to do.

What will people make of the new you.

Truth, is you don't have to care.

Fact is you paid your dues.

You can look how you like and go anywhere.

Does that mean I can be free at my age to be me.

I have no one to impress so long as I'm happy and relaxed about things people will just have to accept the new me, or not whatever the case may be.

Random act of Kindness.

Love the random kindness of people.

Going along the pavement on my electric wheelchair.

To be confronted with my enemy the super-market trolley.

Car stopped man jumped out and moved said trolley.

Apologised for his fellow man.

And he and his friend drove away.

I thanked him very much.

Act of random kindness.

Do you know my shoe size.

You don't even know my shoe size.

So, you haven't walked my path.

Let alone in my footsteps.

As the great 1970s philosopher Lol Crème would say.

Life is a minestrone served up with parmesan cheese.

What would you do.

If you fall from your bike.

Do you climb back on and finish your journey.

Do you decide to walk in the freezing cold.

Do you decide to sit where you are.

Staring at your bike and do nothing.

Wheelchair life is not easy.

The 141 buses from Musselburgh to Penicuik surpassed itself today.

Driver let everyone on the bus before me in my wheelchair.

Result the bus was packed with no room for me to reverse my wheelchair into allocated tiny space.

I asked Gentleman if he would be kind enough to stand to the side for a second so I could reverse my wheelchair, explaining to him I must get the correct angle.

His response I don't see why I should move I have a sore leg you know.

I answered politely sorry to hear that, but the bus won't move until my wheelchair is parked and secure.

His reply was so what.

Me, still calm at this point although a little less calm than before so well if you don't move I can't park my chair so the bus won't be going anywhere.

His response I suppose so but it's a bloody nuisance.

Me I think I deserve a medal for not losing my temper with said man and thanked him for his cooperation.

The joys of wheelchair life.

What can you do.

What can you do when your mind is confused.

Your brain won't work as it used too.

The thoughts get dark they get mixed up.

It's like an overworked fuse that just blew.

The voices you hear you don't recognise.

But whatever they are saying it's not coming from you.

The booze you know will make it worse.

You know deep down that it's just a curse.

A teenager in the 70s

White platform shoes.

Maroon bell bottom trousers.

Cheesecloth Shirts.

Tank Tops.

Long Wavy Hair.

T.Rex. and the Sweet.

Slow dancing to puppy love.

1976 and the sweltering heat.

Colour TV and Remote Control.

Top Of the Pops on a Thursday.

Or a bit of Norther Soul.

We lost Elvis in August 77.

The king of Rock and Roll.

Tomorrow is a new day.

When you're in the library.

And your brain won't work.

Sometimes you must reluctantly accept the fact.

Tomorrow is a new day.

Filled with opportunities and choices.

Coffee books and writing.

For me the only way.

Please just be aware.

You parked your car on the pavement again.

I feel your pain delivering parcels all day.

I will just be 5 minutes you always say.

Long enough for me to miss my bus.

You don't want me to go on the road do you.

You're a decent guy I know you are.

You wouldn't want me to get hit by a car.

Equally I get that you don't want to park too far.

These boxes look heavy,

All I ask is this, be aware of buggies prams and wheelchairs.

When deciding where to park.

Thank you.

The creeping enemy.

Alcohol the enemy that creeps

Up behind you without you noticing him.

And by the time you realise it's there it's too late.

He already has you in a choke hold.

You struggle to break free.

But he is stronger than you thought.

You don't have long to decide your next move.

The nights are the worst.

This cough at night.

Keeping me wide awake.

Making my chest feel tight.

Is as much as I can take.

It's been part of me for so long.

We read the same books.

And listen to the same song.

Will it ever go.

I honestly don't know.

It seems like it is here to say.

Part of me now, it won't go away.

Do you remember.

Do you remember going to your GPs surgery without an appointment it was ran on a first come first serve basis.

Do you remember your GP smoking his pipe or his cigarette at his desk while chatting to you.

Do you remember being ill as a child and while waiting for a home visit your mum would tidy your bedroom get you out of bed to make it before you went back in it.

Do you remember the fish and chip van calling round every week.

Do you remember the Provident man calling on a Friday night and the insurance man on a Saturday morning.

Do you remember having to call your mums friend Aunty even though she wasn't.

Do you remember your dad taking you to the football on a Saturday afternoon and getting a lift over the turnstiles and getting a programme and a pie at half time.

Do you remember when Pubs, Restaurants, Cinemas and even Planes allowed you to smoke cigarettes or even a pipe.

If you remember the above, how old are we?

McDonalds.

This is why I make the effort to go out every morning.

I had no plans, so I headed out to McDonalds
I love the coffee.

I noticed they had put up the price but its half
the cost of other coffee shops.

Met David 68 he moved to Roslin with his
wife from Dundee.

He is a keen cyclist, and we spent an hour
just chatting about everything.

He was a please to be with and get to know.

Love people, love coffee, love life,

Get back up.

If you fall from your horse even though the
pain might be bad

And it seems impossible to stand up and you
look at the size of the horse.

And you think I'm in too much pain I will nev-
er get back on, and you try but

You feel like giving up its just too difficult, but
your life depends on being on that horse.

And riding through life.

Don't give up because that is not an option,

everyone falls now and again but it's how you react to the fall.

Eventually eureka you made it sitting tall and proud of that beautiful horse, just take your time and try not to fall off again.

Daily advice.

You've got to get up every morning.

With determination if you're going

To go to bed with satisfaction.

141 bus it's been a while.

I reintroduced myself with the 141 bus today.

Heart pounding, brow sweating, trying not to fuss.

It's on time, so that's a good sign.

Until I'm on and settled though I know I won't be fine.

The driver smiles the kind of smile that says yes, I have space.

For you and your wheelchair.

The bus is quiet as I get on, only problem is maybe the wheelchair space.

Got narrower, or has my driving got worse,

As I bang into every fixture on the bus.

Eventually after four attempts I reach my goal.

I ask myself about the fuss.

Just to get a wheelchair on a bus

Unless you have tried it you can't possibly know, at least I'm not in a rush.

Where did the grass go.

No grass to weed.

No birds to feed.

No hedge to cut.

No grass to edge.

No flowers to plant.

No not even veg.

No bush to trim.

No shed to clean.

The days gone by.

Are just a dream.

Your mind.

Your mind is with you night and day.

Be careful what you think.

Be careful what you say.

Your thoughts.

Make being alone with your thoughts.

A safe place for you.

From my hospital bed.

Sitting in my hospital bed.

Dealing with the pain.

Mostly physical but some emotional.

Outside its heavy rain.

Patients come and patients go.

But the staff they stay the same.

A conveyor belt that's all it is.

The patient with no name.

Marriage.

Man in the next bed to me (hospital)

Announces I have been married.

To Karen for 49 years.

Me, oh I am terribly sorry.

You have my sincere Sympathy.

(What did I say wrong)

Karen.

Dear Karen.

I know this is hard to hear.

Mere mortals might be filled with fear.

But not you as you bluster on.

Unaware that your rude and entitled.

And you do nothing wrong.

Oh, Karen off you go.

We already guessed that the answer is no.

Karen. Part 2.

It pays to be a Karen,

You often get what you want.

Be a pest be a pain.

And they will do anything.

To never see you again.

Ward 404.

Where old Edinburgh meets new Edinburgh.

Archie 75 years old fae Leith, he is the salt of the earth.

Calls a spade a spade but has a heart of gold.

By his own admission aye, I'm getting old.

Born in bread in Leith.

He laughs at least I still have my own teeth.

So, he says anyway.

Mince and tatties and crumble and custard.

Old school, reading the Edinburgh Evening News.

He blurts out he really misses his wife.

Five years ago, she was taken from his life.

It's really no the same San.

By the way, your no bad considering you're a Hearts fan.

New Edinburgh.

Thomas comes into the ward with his wife.

I guess both in their late 30s.

She scolds the nurse in her middle-class voice.

His name is Thomas not Tam.

The nurse bows her head and sarcastically says, terribly sorry Ma-am.

It is lunchtime and the ward is bedlam.

I feel sorry for Tam, sorry I mean Thomas.

He appears to have lost his voice as Valerie his wife talks on his behalf.

Thomas winces in pain as he sits.

I am trying not to laugh.

As she strokes his arm as if it is for the last time.

Darling it will be ok I am here for you.

He suddenly finds his voice and blurts out honestly, I am fine.

Valerie to the Nurse.

Only one vegetarian option on the lunch menu.

Thomas is vegan so what will you do.

The nurse is speechless and before she can talk.

Valerie announces just as well I brought a packed lunch.

But the food might be an issue.

Archie from the next bed shouts.

He will eat what the rest oh us eat.

But, but, but Thomas can't eat meat.

Sadly, that's where I left old Edinburgh to get on with new Edinburgh.

Printed in Great Britain
by Amazon